LITTLE SPIRO

Books by Ralph Schoenstein:

The Block
Time Lurches On
With T-Shirts and Beer Mugs for All
My Year in the White House Doghouse

LITTLE SPIRO

RALPH
SCHOENSTEIN
editor

ARNOLD
ROTH
art curator

William Morrow and Company, Inc.

New York **1971**

For Judy, Jill, and Eve-Lynn

I did not raise Little Spiro.

—Benjamin Spock

Neither did I.

—Eva Braun

PREFACE

The letters, poems, essays, diary, and songs in this remarkable book are the most dramatic literary find since the discovery of the early graffiti of General Grant. Covering a splendid range of beloved American themes from puberty to law and order, these lyrical childhood flights reveal the total development of the greatest household word of our time.

"We had always hoped for a record like this on Attila the Hun," one Princeton historian told me, "but Attila's teachers threw everything out; and later, of course, he threw *them* out. But the people around Little Spiro were inspired collectors."

It was early one morning in May of 1970, while looking for pre-Columbian treasures, that I stumbled upon these papers in an abandoned laundromat overlooking downtown Detroit, where years of storage in a washer set for gentle action had protected them from the ravages of the atmosphere. Although I have had no formal training in the study of Greco-American juvenalia, I knew at a glance that this was no ordinary find. With trembling hands, I took the papers to the reading room of a nearby Holiday Inn, reverently copied each one, and then framed all the originals for permanent display at both the Smithsonian and Menninger institutions.

I have read each of these papers dozens of times, often to my children when they misbehave, and I now am certain of the wisdom of the poet who said, "The child is the father to the man, unless it's a girl." Needless to say, historians like Professor Kramm, whose brilliantly searching critique follows the pastoral poem entitled "A Little Left Wing," will be plumbing analytical depths that even I haven't been able to reach, while literary critics will be spellbound by a style that blends the simplicity of Hemingway with the spelling of Rudolf Flesch. One must be careful, however, not to *over*analyze these works, for there is less to some of them than meets the eye.

In assembling Little Spiro's papers, which cover the years from 1925 to either 1936 or '41, I was at first unsure about the order in which to arrange them for publication. For a while, it seemed only logical to begin with the ones done in crayon and then move up through pencil to ink; but then I suddenly saw that Little Spiro at seventeen sounded just the way he did at six, when a rare intellectual peak was achieved. So I decided to let the documents fall where they might and devoted myself to numbering the pages, which I finally arranged consecutively from one to ninety-six. For their help in making this arrangement, I am deeply indebted to many hundreds of people.

EDITOR

LITTLE SPIRO

When I Grow Up

When I grow up, I would either like to manage a supermarket in Baltimore or be Vice President of the United States. Of course, I know it takes brains to manage a supermarket.

Little Spiro

My Personally Perfect Pyramid

Dear Dick:

Thank you for your nice letter telling me you have no friends.

Yes, I'll be happy to be your pen pal. I've never known any Quakers, but I'm willing to take a chance.

I think it's terrific that when you grow up, you want to be in middle management.

Your pal,
Little Spiro

The preceding letter is the first in a series sent by Little Spiro to a lonely Quaker boy in California. The Quaker boy's replies are now in the Douglas Mac-Arthur Memorial Collection of the Anaheim branch of the Salvation Army.

Editor

Dear Judy:

You are driving me mad with desire. I stay up half the night wondering how it would feel to unbutton your mackinaw. Pray for me.

Your friend,
Little Spiro

An Effete Snob Sprinkling His Lawn

Dear Miss Smith:

I love the way you sing that new song, "God Bless America."

My friend Herbie says that once in a while God blesses Czechoslovakia too. Is this possible?

Yours truly,
Little Spiro

Dear Dad:

Thank you very much for whacking me with your belt when you caught me with those pictures from the *National Geographic*. I promise I won't ever again look at that part of Tanganyika.

Your son,
Little Spiro

Dear Dad:

Thank you very much for whacking me with your belt when you caught me with that picture of the Washington Monument. I never knew the Monument was *that* kind of symbol, too.

From now on, it's just Grant's Tomb for me.

Your son,
Little Spiro

Pornography on Our Very Streets

All my investigation seems to indicate that Little Spiro wrote the following song for the laying of the corner-stone at the Women's House of Detention.

Editor

My Favorite Things

Haircuts and soldiers and nice party manners,
Waltzes and curfews and maids in bandanas,
Government airplanes with bombs in their wings,
These are a few of my favorite things.

Top commissars who are assassinated,
Hearing the Roosevelt family berated,
Feeling the glow that a good hanging brings,
These are a few of my favorite things.

When the mob strikes
To remove kings
And the left is glad,
I think of a few of my favorite things
And then I don't feel so bad.

Public schoolteachers who still lay on lashes,
Censors who clean college bookstores where trash is,
Chinese who want to go back to the Mings,
These are a few of my favorite things.

My First Chemistry Set

Dear Mr. Hoover:

I don't know if you're the one who runs the FBI
or the Depression, but I want you to know that
I love them both.

Could you please tell me why the FBI shot
Mr. Dillinger coming out of that movie?
It wasn't a dirty picture.

Yours truly,
Little Spiro

My First Beanie

Dear Judy:

I love you but I know nothing about sex and I don't want to know. The only reason I held your hand in the movies was to keep you from clapping for Roosevelt.

Your friend,
Little Spiro

Dear General MacArthur:

    You, Babe Ruth, and Genghis Khan are
my favorite Americans.

    I really got a terrific thrill when you and the
Army gassed all those old bonus veterans who marched
on Washington. Anyway, it was a lousy parade.

Sincerely,
Little Spiro

My Favorite Religious Leader

Clean Is Keen

A child should always say what's true
And speak when he is spoken to,
And keep clean hands and a mind that's cleaner,
Prepared to answer each subpoena.

Dear Lone Ranger:

Do you wear that mask because of a skin condition or because you don't want your Texas friends to see you running around with an Indian?

Yours for policing the plains,
Little Spiro

Although these letters, poems, and essays ostensibly reveal Little Spiro's attitudes toward pornography, country, duty, and dessert, an underlying leitmotif is evident in every word: to wit, the boy's subconscious distress over the loss of a pair of handcuffs that he'd been given for his fifth birthday.

These handcuffs had been a gift from his doting uncle, a Baltimore patrolman not above playing loose with city property, and Little Spiro had taken to them with a penological glee, puckishly slapping them on all his little friends.

And then came the traumatic moment: on the last day of school, Little Spiro took the handcuffs to class for show-and-tell and merrily placed them on the wrists of a certain young lady who'd been praising Social Security; but then a fire drill was held and when Little Spiro returned to the room, both the girl and the handcuffs were gone. He has spent the rest of his life subconsciously looking for them and yearning to see American women kept in their place.

Dr. Arnold M. Siegel
Consulting Psychologist
Kiwanis Club of Philadelphia

The Founding Fathers Working on the First Amendment

Dear Dick:

   It was great to hear from you again. And it was sure swell of you to send me all those football scores. I really enjoyed them, but next time could you send me a sentence or two?

                          Your pal,
                          Little Spiro

Dear Tarzan:

I really love the way you swing from trees
and shape up the apes and keep law and order in
the jungle. It makes me proud that you're an
American.

Please write back if you know how.

Your fan,
Little Spiro

The Slaves

The slaves came over from Africa because America was a land of opportunity. A few of the slaves ran into prejudice, but most of them were allowed to go right to work.

*The Melting Pot: A Place for Everybody
and Everybody in His Place*

A Song of Love

My Bonnie lies over the ocean,
My Bonnie lies over the sea,
But she never lies to committees
On internal security.

My First Two-Wheeler

Dear Father Coughlin:

I hear that you have a swell radio show. I would love to get into broadcasting myself some day, so could you please send me the information about how to do it.

Do you just talk about patriotic things on your show or do you also give the sports and weather too?

Sincerely,
Little Spiro

Dear Martha:

Thanks for inviting me to the KKK hop, but I'm afraid I can't come. I got pretty dirty at Halloween and my mother won't give me another sheet.

Your friend,
Little Spiro

My Second Beanie (Prewar)

Dear Dick:

Your last letter was so great that all I can say is Loyola 20, Fordham 0.

What do you mean that you're not sure you want to go through puberty? If it's something dirty, please call me up and tell me all about it. Don't put anything in the mail.

Your pal,
Little Spiro

My Favorite All-Time All-American

Christopher Columbus

Christopher Columbus sailed to the New World in
1492. There he found people with syphilis whom he
called Indians.

Dear Mr. Disney:

I just saw your new picture, *Snow White and the Seven Dwarfs*, and I do not think that those seven miners are an accurate picture of the American working man. They are much too interested in that teen-age girl. And they also do strange things with animals.

Yours truly,

Little Spiro

A Pusillanimous Pussyfooter

Dear Miss Temple:

I love your singing and dancing and the adorable way that you play with dolls and Negroes.

Your fan,
Little Spiro

My Philosophy

Roses are red,
Violets are blue,
Reporters are pink,
Beware of what's new.

The preceding verse reveals Little Spiro's deep distrust of the American news media. He did have a newspaper route, but feeling that most of the paper was "fish-wrapping rhetoric," he delivered only the sports section and the part of the radio page that listed Gabriel Heatter.

Editor

Dear Mr. Lindbergh:

What a terrific flight!

But why did you go to Paris, which has all those students and fairies?

Next time please make it Des Moines.

Sincerely,
Little Spiro

Lucky Lindy's Lascivious Landing

Dear Billy:

It was great having you visit me for the Christmas holidays.

I know all that stuff that you told me came from your Sunday school, but it's still hard for me to believe that Jesus was a Jew. Are you *really sure*? There's a family down the street named Magdalene, so he *could* have been an American, couldn't he?

                                        Your pal,
                                        Little Spiro

Dear Dick:

We are having a debate here at school called "Should We Take the Marines Out of Nicaragua?" and I am going to be in it.

Would you please tell me everything you know about Nicaragua. I like bananas but I don't think that's enough.

> Your pal,
> Little Spiro

Dear Dick:

Thanks for all the swell stuff on Nicaragua. I never knew that it belongs to the United States.

I will try to take your advice about the debate and be on both sides, but I think we're supposed to take one or the other.

That's very exciting news about your sincerity lessons. My parents want me to take piano.

> Your pal,
> Little Spiro

My Sports Beanie

Dear Duke of Windsor:

Congratulations on trading the British Empire for a woman from Baltimore. You made a terrific deal. My mother is a woman from Baltimore and I wouldn't trade her for Canada, India, and Boardwalk with two hotels.

Your fan,
Little Spiro

Dear Mom and Dad:

  Scout camp is terrific this year. I was really
getting tired of the Boy Scouts and that's why I'm
glad you sent me over here on an international
exchange. Mr. Mussolini says that if we keep up
the good work, he'll let us all go camping in Ethiopia.

                              Your son,
                              Little Spiro

Capital Punishment

I am in favor of capital punishment because it really teaches those killers a lesson they'll never forget.

My First Erector Set

Brotherhood Week

I'm really in favor of Brotherhood Week,
When every Polack is as good as a Greek.
And unless every Wop is as good as a Jap,
Brotherhood is a lot of crap.

My Diary

Dear Diary:

The other kids in the class keep raising their hands to leave the room, but I think all this permissiveness is a dangerous drift to the left. I just stay in my seat and squirm for my country.

Permissiveness

The Depression

A lot of people in this country are now out of work and standing around selling apples, but this is what makes our system so great. In Soviet Russia, no one would have the incentive to sell apples or even tangerines because the state handles all the fruit.

Free Enterprise System Being Saved
Not a Minute Too Soon

A Little Left Wing

A birdie with a yellow bill
Hopped upon my windowsill,
Cocked his shining eye and said,
"The robin is a dirty red."

The editor has asked me to discuss the historical symbolism of the preceding poem. I don't know what the hell he's talking about, but I'll take a fling at it anyway because I have a feeling that Little Spiro may some day be a legitimate public figure.

In analyzing the first line of the poem, "A birdie with a yellow bill," I quite agree with Professor Springer of Yale, who says that this line is an obvious metaphor for the American eagle demanding payment of a debt by the defaulting Chinese.

In the poem's second line, "Hopped upon my windowsill," the eagle has come directly to Little Spiro for help in carrying out the American mission in Asia. Crows and pigeons also stopped at his room, but they perched there with no significance.

The third line of the poem, "Cocked his shining eye and said," is a maddeningly enigmatic one because it seems to be a non-sequitur about gun control. Moreover, Springer feels that the line as we have it here may very well be a misprint, that originally it may have been written as "Hocked his shining eye and said," words with which Little Spiro might have been trying to describe a sellout of the American Dream.

Many scholars choose to completely ignore line four, and who can take them to task?

There is, needless to say, another possible interpretation of the entire poem based on the use of "bill" at the beginning. Some of us have every reason to believe that during her pregnancy, Little Spiro's mother was badly frightened by the Bill of Rights.

G. Wilfred Kramm
American Legion Professor of History
University of Nevada at Las Vegas

My Favorite Sport

Our Constitution

The Constitution of the United States is okay except for the part about promoting the general welfare. Those founding fathers had no business starting relief.

The Welfare System Getting Out of Hand

My First Real Hat

Dear Santa:

Please bring me a set of dominoes.

Yours truly,
Little Spiro

Dear Mr. Mayor:

I think it's a disgrace the way people sit on flagpoles these days. It's not just unpatriotic but it makes it very hard to get the flag to the top.

Yours truly,
Little Spiro

Dear Dick:

What do you mean that getting an allowance is inflationary?

Your pal,
Little Spiro

One of My Ancestors Inventing Democracy

Dear Dick:

I just read a new book called *The Grapes of Wrath*, which is about a bunch of bums who left Oklahoma to go on relief in California. I hope that none of them ruined your neighborhood.

Your pal,
Little Spiro

The Birds

In the winter birds go south, where there are free elections.

My Favorite Bird

Dear Mr. Kipling:

I am doing a term paper on the white man's burden and I wonder if you could send me some information about it. Please tell me all the colors that white men are better than.

Sincerely,
Little Spiro

My Favorite Statue

My Future Beanie

Dear Mr. President:

In spite of what happened at Pearl Harbor yesterday, I see no need for America to rush into a war with a country that has such a low rate of juvenile delinquency.

Sincerely,

Little Spiro

The Younger Generation Ruining Our Country

INDEX

Ralph Schoenstein

Born in New York City in 1933, Ralph Schoenstein attended Hamilton College, where a hyperthyroid condition led him to become head cheerleader, and Columbia College, where he missed Phi Beta Kappa by a wide margin. He served without distinction in the Army and then, inspired by a liberalization of unemployment insurance, began free-lance writing. He has been a columnist for two defunct newspapers, an essayist on four television networks, and the author of five books and hundreds of magazine pieces. He is a correspondent for *Punch*, and his work appears in ten anthologies, all best sellers. He was the first writer arrested at the Democratic Convention in Chicago, where he went to jail two nights before it became fashionable. He lives in Princeton with his wife, Judy, and his daughters, Jill and Eve-Lynn. He has no connection with the intellectual life of the community.

Arnold Roth

Born in Philadelphia in 1929, Arnold Roth attended the Philadelphia College of Art, from which he was expelled in 1948. Working as a free-lance artist since 1951, he has won awards in almost every Art Director and Illustrator's Exhibit in America. A former professional saxophone player and a rising pool hustler, he draws a feature called "Roth's America" for *Punch* and has contributed to almost every national magazine except *Think* and *Cattleman's Quarterly*. He has done illustrations for more than a dozen books (two more), including *Pick a Peck of Puzzles* (which he also wrote), *Houseful of Laughter, The President's Mystery Plot, Isabel's Noel, Grimm's Fairy Tales,* and *The Inchworm War and the Butterfly Peace*. Married to the former Caroline Wingfield, he is the father of two sons, Charles and Adam. He lives in Princeton not far from Ralph Schoenstein, who says, "Not far enough."